OPTICAL ILLUSIONS
BRAIN BUSTERS

GIANNI A. SARCONE AND MARIE-JO WAEBER

Quarto is the authority on a wide range of topics.

Quarto educates, entertains and enriches the lives of our readers—enthusiasts and lovers of hands-on living.

www.quartoknows.com

Concepts, text, and research: Gianni A. Sarcone

Design and Editorial: Tall Tree Ltd
Project Editor: Harriet Stone

This library edition published in 2019
by Quarto Library,
an imprint of The Quarto Group.
6 Orchard Road
Suite 100
Lake Forest, CA 92630
T: +1 949 380 7510
F: +1 949 380 7575
www.QuartoKnows.com

A CIP record for this book is available from the Library of Congress.

SBN 978-0-71124-228-9
Manufactured in Dongguan, China TL012019
9 8 7 6 5 4 3 2 1

Words in **bold** are explained in the glossary on page 23.

CONTENTS

IS SEEING BELIEVING?

Can you really believe what you see? This book will show you some amazing illusions that will trick your eyes and brain. It also contains simple experiments to show you how you can make your own incredible illusions.

How You See

At the front of your head are two forward-facing jelly balls, called your eyes. Rays of light are bent as they pass through the cornea and enter your eye through a tiny peephole, called the pupil. The lens bends the light rays a little more to focus them, before they pass through the middle of the eye and hit the **retina**, the lining at the back of each eyeball. As light hits the retina, it stimulates millions of light-sensitive cells, called **photoreceptors**. These send electrical nerve signals along the optic nerve to the back of the brain and a part called the visual cortex. This produces the final images that you see.

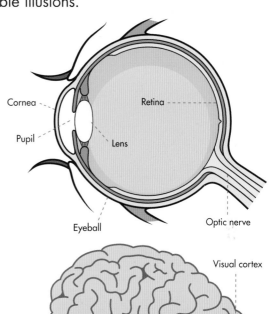

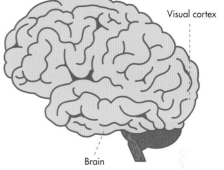

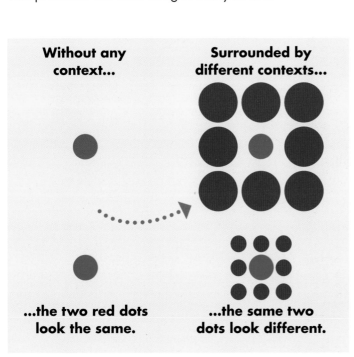

Without any context...

Surrounded by different contexts...

...the two red dots look the same.

...the same two dots look different.

Context

While that all sounds nice and scientific, your seeing equipment can sometimes be fooled into seeing things that aren't there, or incorrectly seeing things that are there. These effects are called optical illusions. Many illusions are created because we don't see objects on their own. Instead, we see them in context and surrounded by other objects which can influence how we see things.

THE BRAIN

Without the active involvement of your brain, you would probably see the world as monochromatic (in one color), upside-down, and with a large hole in the middle.

Your brain is great at filling in gaps in your vision. You may be surprised to learn that there is a hole in the back of each of your eyes. This hole is called the **"blind spot"** and it is where the optic nerve enters the eyeball to connect it to the brain. You don't usually notice this blind spot because your brain is able to reorganize or restore an image to cover up this hole! Your brain applies "conformation," using incomplete shapes to create lines or **contours** to fill in the gaps. These are known as **contour illusions**.

What can you see between these black shapes?

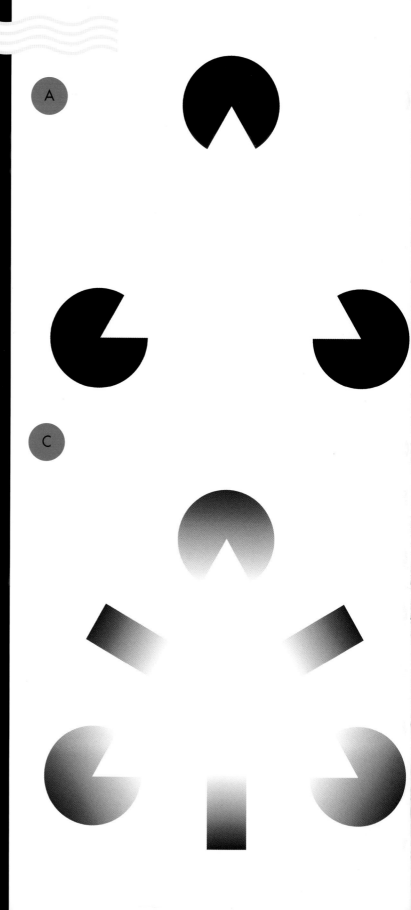

Pac-Man
Illusion

The Pac-Man shapes in image A give an illusion of a bright white triangle. When the Pac-Man shapes are rotated (image B), the illusion disappears.

what's going on?

In image A, your brain uses the information it is given to form contours that complete the shape: a triangle. This visual effect can be enhanced by adding a gray gradient to the shapes (image C). Now the triangle appears to have a halo around it! In image D, you should be able to see a cat playing with a butterfly, even though the shapes are incomplete. Your brain adds in the missing contours, making the shapes fit with other mental structures that are stored in your mind.

Contours and **3-D Shapes**

See how these 2-D patterns can create the impression of 3-D shapes.

This image looks like a 3-D ball covered with spikes. Even though the overall shape is flat and without contours, your brain interprets the black patterns as spikes sticking out of a sphere!

This looks like a spotted 3-D spring, but where are its contours? In fact, this spring could never exist, because it is only formed from floating colored disks and semicircles.

Colors Affect **Contours**

The illusions on this page will show you how colors can produce contour effects.

In the pictures above, you may see a pale gray disk in the circle on the left and a bright disk in the circle on the right, even though both backgrounds are white.

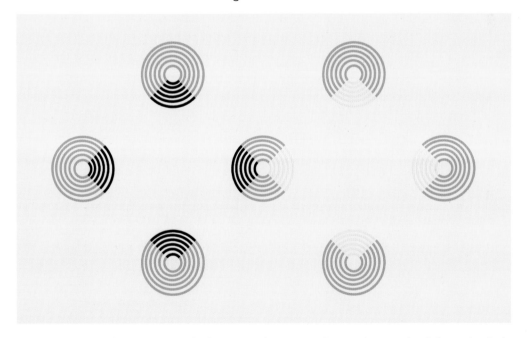

You should be able to see a dark square between the circles on the left and a lighter square between the circles on the right, even though the color is the same as the background.

what's going on?

In these illusions, the contours are being created by the different colors in the squares and circles. The different colors also affect the tone of the created shapes, with lighter colors producing lighter shapes, and darker colors producing darker shapes.

Geometric Illusion

See how arranging these simple geometric
shapes can make part of an object "disappear."

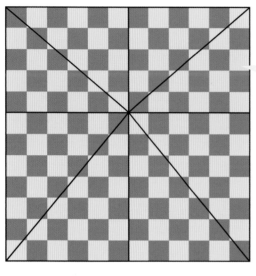

1 Trace the two large squares
shown here and cut them
along the black lines to make
12 triangle and square pieces.

2 Arrange these pieces to form square A shown
below. Then rearrange the shapes to show
square B. Part of the square appears to have
disappeared, even though you're using the
same shapes and the squares are the same size!

A

B

what's going on?

Actually, square A is not really a square but a slightly concave
shape, whose edges curve inward. Square B with a square hole
in its center is slightly convex and its edges curve outward. So the
missing section is simply spread along the edges of the square.

Aftereffects

"**Aftereffects**" are visual illusions that appear after your eyes are exposed to a stimulus for a long period of time. There are many types of aftereffects. Color aftereffects are usually called **afterimages**.

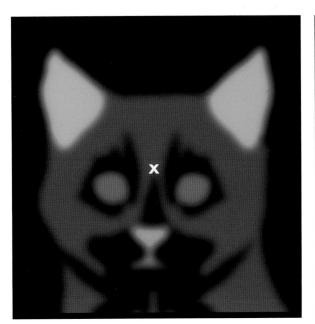

Can you make the black-and-white image of the cat turn full-color?

Stare at the small white cross in the colored image for about 30 seconds. Then quickly shift your gaze to the black-and-white image.

When you now look at the cat on the right, it will appear colorful, but with different colors to the cat on the left.

what's going on?

Staring at a color for a long period of time will produce an afterimage in a **complementary color**. Examples of complementary colors are red and green, purple and yellow, and blue and orange. So staring at the blue color in the image on the left will create an aftereffect of orange when you look at the image on the right.

Blurred **Face**

Find out how you can make pin-sharp photos look blurry with this simple illusion.

Stare at the pale star between the upper pair of faces for about 20–30 seconds, then quickly look at the star in the middle of the lower pair of pictures.

You will notice that for just a few seconds the image of the woman on the left will look more blurred than the right one in the bottom pair, even though they are identical.

what's going on?

The illusion comes from a visual aftereffect that scientists call "contrast adaptation" or "contrast gain control." It shows that when you look at blurred or unfocused images for a long time, it can affect how you see other objects.

The Mischievous Leprechaun

1 2 3 4 5 6

Can you make the leprechaun disappear?

Hold the page about 12 inches in front of you. Close your left eye and focus with your right eye on each number from six to one, one at a time. Count down as you do this and by the time you get to three, the leprechaun will appear to have wandered off the circle.

what's going on?

The blind spot in each of your eyes has no light-sensitive cells, or photoreceptors. So when the image of the leprechaun enters your blind spot he seems to disappear! French scientist Edme Mariotte was the first person to talk about the blind spot in humans in 1660.

Cheshire **Cat**

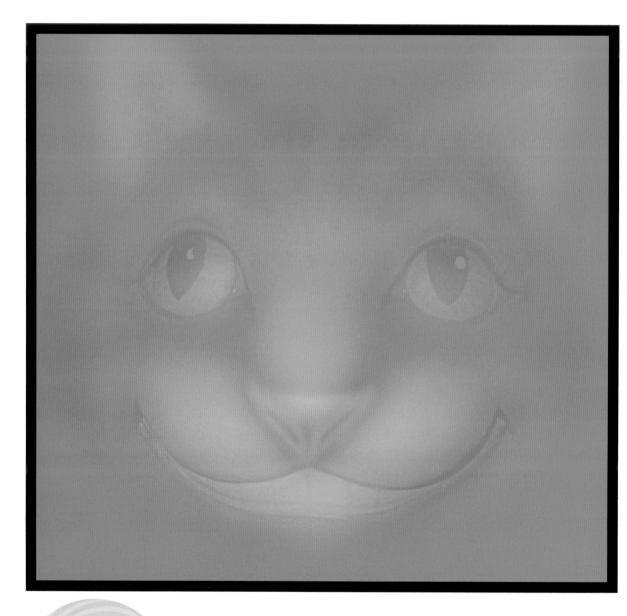

Stare at this cat's nose and count to 20. Watch as the face disappears.

what's going on?

The brown and green colors of the cat are very poor at stimulating your vision, so the image of the cat will appear to fade. Moving your eyes around will restore the image.

Impossible **Triangle**

Challenge your friends to create this seemingly impossible triangle from a sheet of paper. Then follow these steps to show them how it's done!

WHAT YOU NEED
- Sheet of paper
- Pair of scissors

1

Make a short crease across the middle of the paper by pinching the central part only.

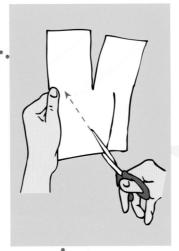

2

Reopen the sheet and make a right-angled cut from the middle of one edge to the center crease. Then make two cuts to form a V-shape from the opposite edge as shown.

3

Finally, turn the right flap of the sheet forward 180 degrees and the triangle piece should stand upright.

what's going on?

It is amazing how many people aren't able to make this 3-D triangle! The mental block is caused by the fact that we perceive the paper as just a 2-D shape rather than a 3-D object that can be moved and altered.

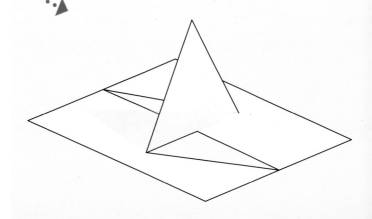

Broken **Plate?**

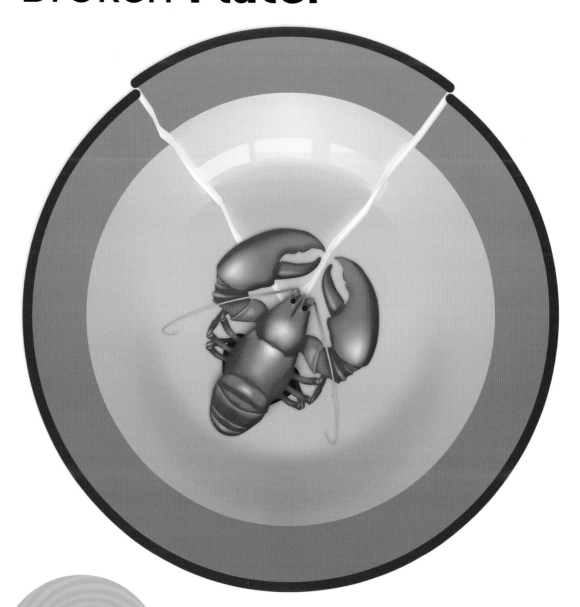

Stare at the lobster's eyes for about 20 seconds and see what happens to the broken plate.

After a while, the rim of the plate will appear to fix itself!

what's going on?

This effect occurs because your brain tends to "iron out" broken lines in your **peripheral vision** without you realizing it.

Stereograms;
3-D Wonders

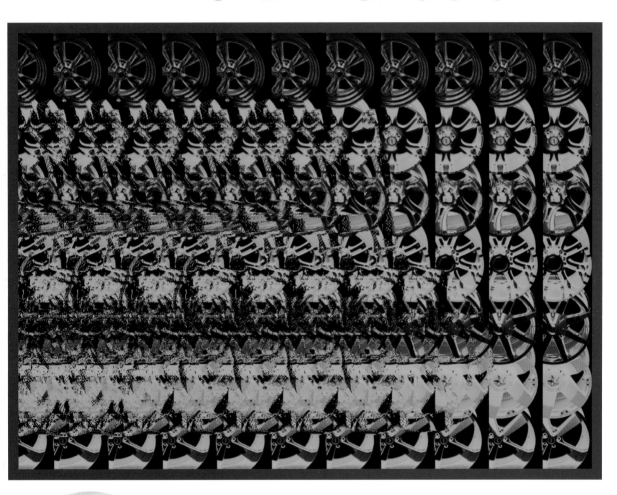

Stare at this colored pattern. Does a 3-D shape appear out of the page?

Stereograms (also known as "autostereograms" or "magic eye") are 3-D images hidden within a 2-D pattern. In order to see the 3-D image, bring the picture close to your eyes, until it touches your nose. At this distance, your eyes cannot focus on the image and they focus somewhere behind the image. Now, slowly move the image away from you, while trying to keep your eyes out-of-focus until you see the hidden image. Seeing a stereogram is tricky and you may have to be patient because it can take a little time.

Leaning **Towers**

Were these two photos taken from the same angle?

The towers appear to be leaning more in image A. But the two photos are exactly the same—yet they seem different! You can see proof of this on page 22.

what's going on?

Both photos have the same **perspective** and the same **vanishing point**. But when they are placed next to each other, your brain interprets them as a single scene with two different vanishing points and it gets confused by the rules of perspective. The leaning effect occurs because the two vanishing points are interpreted as **divergent**, which is why the tower on the left appears to lean more than the one on the right.

A **Confusing** Sign

Which way do the fingers point? Confuse your friends with this topological puzzle.

WHAT YOU NEED
- Sheet of paper
- Colored pencils
- Pair of scissors
- Wooden craft stick
- Glue

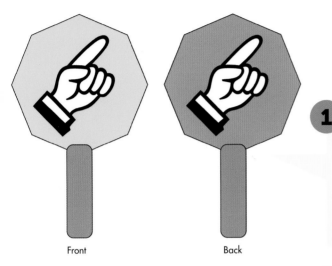

Front   Back

1

Copy the pointing fingers and colored backgrounds shown here onto paper and cut out the octagons. Glue them back-to-back to the end of a wooden craft stick to create your pointing sign.

2

Then ask someone to guess which direction the finger at the back of the sign points when the sign is upright and tilted at 45 or 90 degrees. This is not so obvious and your audience may be surprised at the results.

3

When the sign is tilted at 45 degrees, the finger at the back of the sign points at a right-angle to the finger on the front! And when the sign is tilted at 90 degrees, the finger is pointing in the opposite direction.

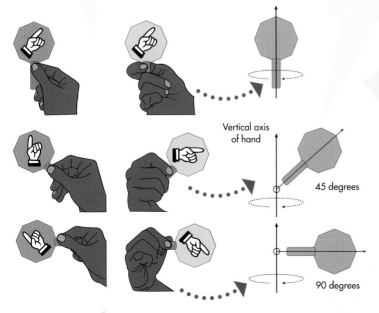

Vertical axis of hand

45 degrees

90 degrees

what's going on?

To understand why this happens, you have to think about the vertical axis of your hand holding the sign, and the axis of the sign's handle. Rotating your hand moves the axis of the sign, making the fingers appear to point in different directions.

Disrupting Patterns

What's hidden in this black-and-white image?

This black-and-white image contains a black-and-white Dalmatian dog lying on a black-and-white spotted rug (turn to page 22 to see it more clearly).

what's going on?

The dog and the background have been obscured to show how prior knowledge of an object can help you understand an image. For example, you can't see the outline of the dog so you don't recognize it in the image. **Disruptive patterns** like this often occur in nature. The black-and-white stripes of zebras confuse predators because they cannot focus on an individual animal to catch.

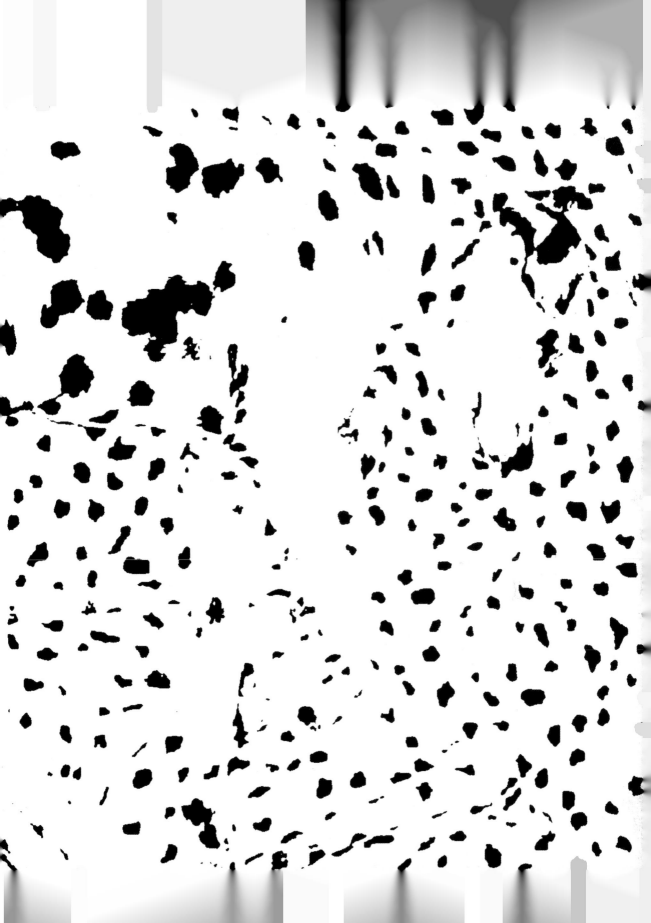

Spot **the Difference**

Can you spot any differences between these women? Turn the book upside-down to check.

When you turn the book around, the woman with the blue glasses looks strange because her mouth and eyes are upside-down!

what's going on?

Your brain is used to seeing faces the right way up, and it is only able to detect small changes in a face in relation to the position of the eyes, the mouth, and the nose. When the face is upside-down, your brain cannot process it properly. The interesting part is that the brain thinks it can, so you see everything as correct, until the image is turned around. This illusion is called the "Thatcher illusion" after former British Prime Minister Margaret Thatcher. Her photo was used to first create this effect by Professor Peter Thompson of the University of York (UK).

A **Toilet Tube** "Squircle"

In this 3-D illusion you will experiment with an idea based on the "cylinder illusion" by Japanese engineer Kokichi Sugihara. This particular shape, known as a "squircle," blends together the shape of a square with the shape of a circle.

WHAT YOU NEED

- Cardboard cylinder (toilet tube)
- Pencil
- Pair of scissors
- Mirror

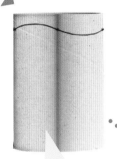

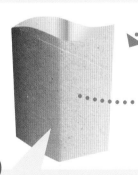

1 Squash your cylinder to make a flat shape. Then open it back out, turn it so that one of the fold lines is running down the center, and squash it again. Mark three dots about one inch from the top, one on the center fold, and the other two on the outer folds.

2 Using these three points as markers, draw a wavy line. Then, cut the cylinder along that line.

3 Now you have a shape with curved edges, halfway between a rhomboid (square) and a hollow cylinder.

4 Place this shape in front of a mirror and arrange it so that the magic happens! As your brain tends to "correct" what you see according to your viewpoint, you will see a perfect rhomboid with corners and its reflection as a perfect cylinder.

These pictures reveal the mysteries of
the illusions from earlier in this book.

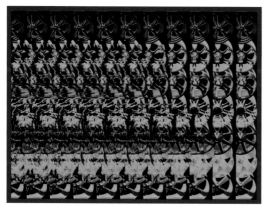

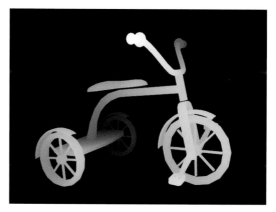

PAGE 15

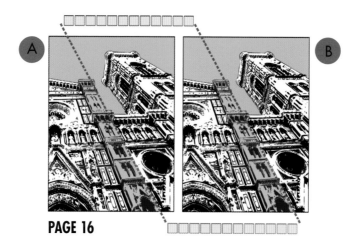

PAGE 16

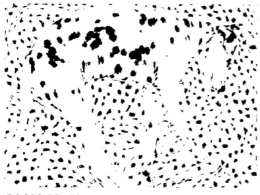

PAGES 18–19

GLOSSARY

aftereffect
An illusion created by your senses being exposed to a stimulus for a long period of time. Color aftereffects are usually called afterimages (see below). Other aftereffects include a feeling of movement caused by staring at a moving object for a while and then looking at a still one.

afterimage
This occurs when you look at brightly colored images for a long period of time. The bright colors desensitize part of your retina at the back of the eye. When you look away or at a neutral surface, such as a white page, a ghostly version of the same image appears, but with different colors.

blind spot
The part of the retina where the optic nerve leaves the eyeball and where there are no photoreceptors. This creates a small area where you cannot see anything. Usually, your brain fills in this blind spot so that you do not notice it.

complementary colors
These are colors that are directly opposite each other on a color wheel, such as red and green or blue and orange. When placed next to each other, these colors can create a vibrant optical effect.

contour
The apparent edge of an object.

contour illusions
The impression of the edge, or contour, of an object that is created by other, incomplete shapes.

desensitizes
Reduces the effect of something, such as a bright light or a particular color.

disruptive patterns
Complicated patterns that are designed to break up the shape of an object. These patterns can hide an object against its background, such as a soldier's camouflaged uniform, or they can be dazzling to confuse somebody watching, such as the bright stripes on a zebra.

divergent
When two or more objects are moving or leaning away from each other.

peripheral vision
The edges of your vision and the areas you can see out of the corners of your eyes.

perspective
The principle that objects will appear to get smaller the farther away they are. Perspective is defined by the horizon or by eye level and by vanishing points.

photoreceptors
Light-sensitive cells in the retinas at the backs of your eyes. They are triggered when rays of light fall on them and send signals to the brain, which turns these signals into the pictures you see.

retina
The thin layer at the back of the eye that covers nearly three-quarters of the inside of the eyeball. It contains millions of light-sensitive photoreceptors.

vanishing point
An imaginary point on the horizon where the perspective lines of buildings and other objects come together, or converge. As they get closer to a vanishing point, objects appear to get smaller and smaller, until they completely disappear.

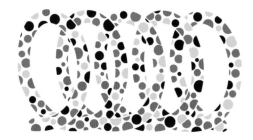

INDEX

PICTURE CREDITS

(t=top, b=bottom, l=left, r=right, c=center)

Dreamstime:
3t © Alexander Pokusay | Dreamstime.com, 3c © Suriya Siritam | Dreamstime.com

Shutterstock:
1 © Shutterstock/casejustin, 21tl & 21tc © iMoved Studio.

All other images courtesy of **Gianni A. Sarcone**.